3.95

LIFE CYCLES

The Frog

Diana Noonan

CHELSEA CLUBHOUSE

An Imprint of Chelsea House Publishers
A Haights Cross Communications ⌐ Company

Philadelphia

Chelsea Clubhouse
1974 Sproul Road, Suite 400
Broomall, PA 19008-0914

The Chelsea House world wide web address is www.chelseahouse.com

Library of Congress Cataloging-in-Publication Data

Noonan, Diana.
   The frog / by Diana Noonan.
   p. cm. — (Life cycles)

   Summary: An introduction to the physical characteristics, behavior, and development from egg to adult of frogs, amphibians that hibernate in the cold.

   ISBN 0-7910-6966-4
   1. Frogs—Life cycles—Juvenile literature. [1. Frogs.] I. Title. II. Series.
   QL668.E2 N66 2003
   597.8'9—dc21

                                                                              2002000034

First published in 1999 by
MACMILLAN EDUCATION AUSTRALIA PTY LTD
627 Chapel Street, South Yarra, Australia, 3141

Copyright © Diana Noonan 1999
Copyright in photographs © individual photographers as credited

Edited by Anne McKenna
Text design by Polar Design
Cover design by Linda Forss

Printed in China

Acknowledgements
Cover: The male red-eyed tree frog stretches its vocal sacs to call to its mate. (A.N.T. Photo Library)

A.N.T. Photo, pp. 4 © S. Wilson, 5 © Otto Rogge, 6 © Jon Hanger, 8, 13, 30 © Klaus Uhlenhut, 9 © J. Frazier, 10, 11 © Dave Watts, 1, 12 © Andrew Dennis, 14, 21, 27, 30 © Ken Griffiths, 15, 19, 20 © N.H.P.A., 16 © Norbert Wu, 17 © D. Clyne, 18 © M.J. Tyler 22, 23, 24, 26, 30 © C. & S. Pollitt, 29 © G.E. Schmida; Auscape, pp. 7 © Joe Mcdonald, 25 © Kathie Atkinson, 28 © Roger Brown.

While every care has been taken to trace and acknowledge copyright, the publisher tenders their apologies for any accidental infringement where copyright has proved untraceable.

Contents

Life Cycles

All animals change as they live and grow. They begin life as tiny creatures. They grow into adults that will produce their own young. The frog has its own special life cycle.

Frogs Are Amphibians

Frogs belong to a group of animals called amphibians. Amphibians can live on land and in water.

Keeping Warm

Amphibians are cold-blooded animals. Their bodies are the same temperature as the air or water around them.

Hibernation

Frogs **hibernate** when the temperature is too cold. Some hibernate under stones or in mud at the bottom of a pond. Some dig a hole in a moist bank.

Breathing

Frogs breathe air through their **lungs**. They also breathe through their moist skin. To keep their skin moist, frogs live in damp places or close to water.

The water-holding frog makes an underground nest. It comes out to mate when it rains.

Frogs that live in hot, dry places sometimes seek shelter under the sand. They dig moist underground nests where they can hide.

Feet and Legs

Frogs that spend time in water have **webbed** back feet to help them swim.

webbed feet

suckers

Tree frogs have **suckers** on their toes to help them climb. Frogs that spend time underground have claws on their toes to help them dig.

Courting

Most frogs **court**, or look for a partner, in spring. The male frog croaks to tell females that he is nearby. He stretches his **vocal sacs** to make his mating call louder.

vocal sac

A male frog calls to its mate.

Mating

The male frog rests on the female frog's back to **mate**. He holds onto her with his front legs. Some male frogs have special pads on their feet. The pads help them hold onto the female's slippery skin.

These frogs are mating.

Laying Eggs

As the female lays her eggs, the male covers them with **sperm** from his body. A jelly-like substance covers each egg.

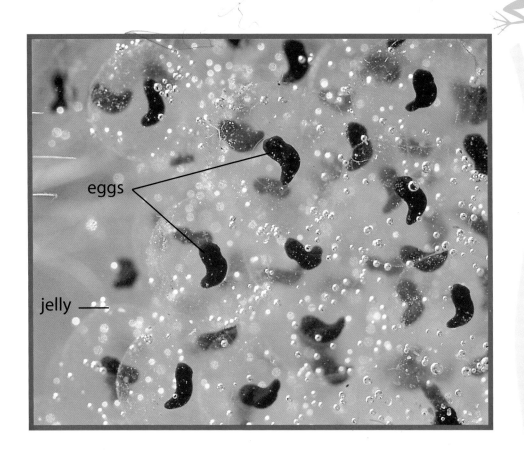

eggs

jelly

The eggs look like tiny black dots. They become longer and curved as they grow. The warmer the conditions, the faster the eggs develop.

Different types of frogs lay eggs in different places. Some frogs lay their eggs on leaves or on the bark of trees.

Some frogs lay eggs on leaves.

A frog laid this clump of eggs in water.

Some frogs make bubbly egg nests that hang from branches. Frogs that live in ponds lay hundreds of eggs in clumps in the water.

Guarding the Eggs

Some frogs keep their eggs in a breeding pouch on their bodies. The frogs look after the eggs as they develop. Other frogs guard their eggs by hatching them in a special stomach. The young froglets then climb out of their parent's mouth.

This froglet hatched in its parent's stomach.

The pond frog does not guard its eggs.
It leaves them in the water to hatch on
their own.

Hatching

Some eggs hatch into tiny frogs. Most hatch into tadpoles first. The tadpoles live in the water while they change into frogs.

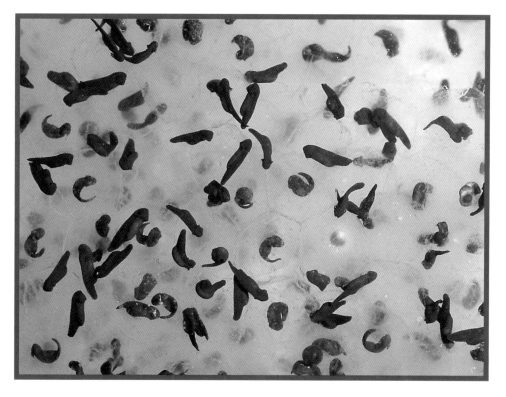

Tadpoles hatch from eggs.

Tadpoles
Tail

A tadpole looks like a small fish. It has a tail to help it swim.

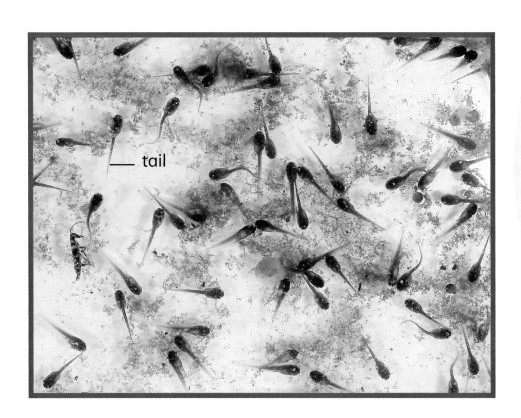

tail

Gills

A tadpole has feathery **gills** behind its head to help it breathe underwater. Later, its gills grow inside its body. Young tadpoles eat pond **algae** in the water.

tail

gills

Legs

The tadpole grows two back legs. It uses these legs to catch small pond animals to eat.

back leg

tail

Lungs

The tadpole stops using its gills after it grows front legs. It swims to the surface to breathe air through its lungs.

front leg

back legs

tail

The Growing Tadpole

The tadpole begins to look more and more like a frog. Its eyes get bigger. Its mouth gets wider.

tail

back leg

front leg

The tadpole's tongue begins to grow. Its tail starts to get shorter. Now it swims by kicking with its back legs.

Froglets

The tadpole's tail becomes a stump. Now the tadpole is called a froglet. It comes out of the water to sit in damp places. It spends its time eating and growing.

stump

Predators

Predators catch and eat frogs and froglets. A frog's skin color helps it hide in its surroundings. But herons and other water birds still catch many frogs and froglets.

Herons catch and eat frogs.

A dragonfly eats a tadpole.

Frogs' eggs and tadpoles are also in danger. Water beetles, dragonflies, and other small animals eat the eggs. Fish eat tadpoles. A frog lays thousands of eggs in its lifetime. But only a few will hatch into tadpoles and grow into adults.

The Life Cycle of a Frog

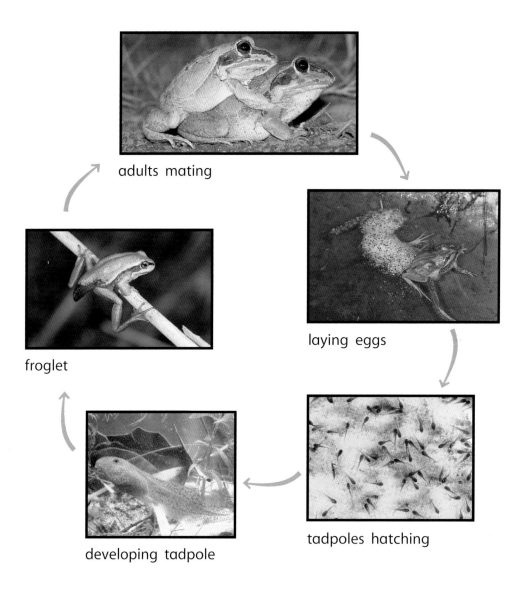

adults mating

laying eggs

froglet

developing tadpole

tadpoles hatching

Glossary

algae small plants without roots or stems that grow in water

court to try to attract a mate

gills the organs on the sides of an animal that help it breathe underwater

hibernate to go into a deep sleep, usually while the temperature is very cold

lungs organs inside the body that frogs and other animals use to breathe

mate to join with a breeding partner to produce young

predator an animal that hunts other animals for food

sperm liquid from a male's body that fertilizes a female's eggs

suckers cup-like parts of the feet that help an animal cling to a surface through suction

vocal sacs stretchy organs at the side of a frog's mouth or beneath its chin that help to make its voice louder

web a flat piece of skin that connects toes or fingers

Index